In this comic ..

CW01073048

Superman

Batman

Chip

Superdog

Princess

The Flash

Jumpa

Ace

Green
Lantern

Aquaman

Streaky

Topo

Beppo

The Super-Pets fly in ...

Force Kanjar to cancel this curse!

We will!

We promise.

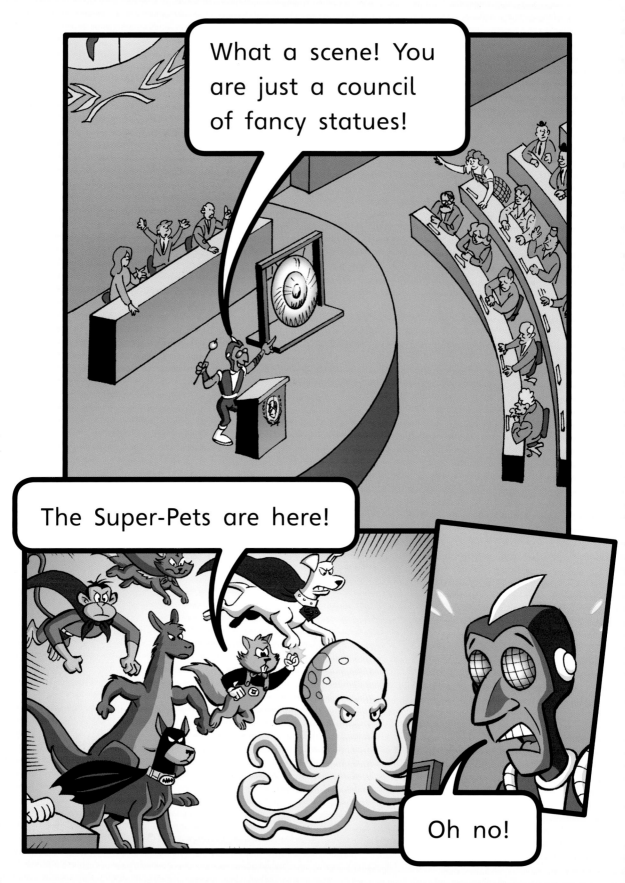

Princess shouts for help.

13

14